Just for Two

A Collection of 8 Piano Duets in a Variety of Styles and Moods
Specially Written to Inspire, Motivate, and Entertain

DENNIS ALEXANDER

My *Just for You* piano solo collections were some of the first books that I wrote for Alfred Music Publishing Company. They have always been among the top sellers in my library. Now, I am delighted to share with you duet versions of many favorites from those solo books in my new series, *Just for Two*. Piano students always enjoy making music together. I hope that these duets will prove to be "twice the fun" of the original solo versions!

Enjoy, and happy music making.

Dennis Alexander

CONTENTS

Alfred Music
P.O. Box 10003
Van Nuys, CA 91410-0003
alfred.com

ISBN-10: 0-7390-8799-1
ISBN-13: 978-0-7390-8799-2

AUTUMN SPLENDOR
Secondo

Dennis Alexander

AUTUMN SPLENDOR
Primo

Dennis Alexander

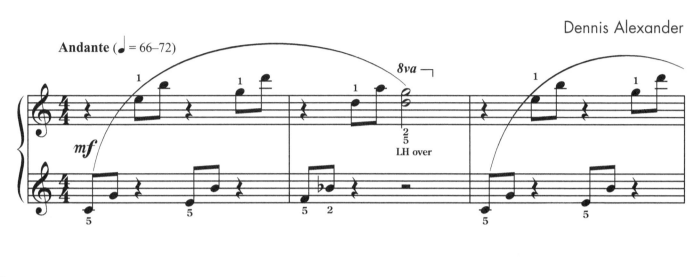

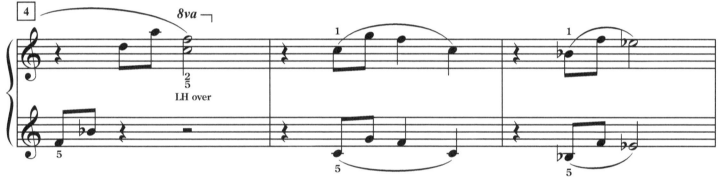

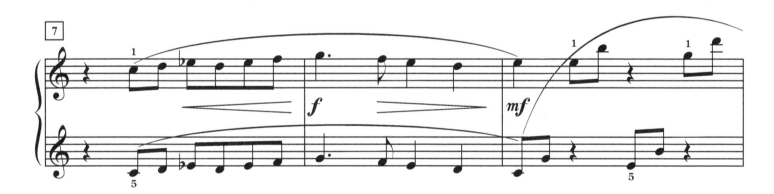

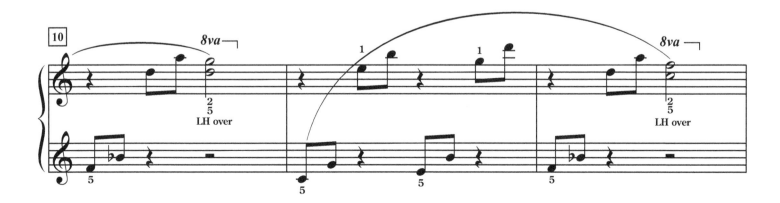

Secondo

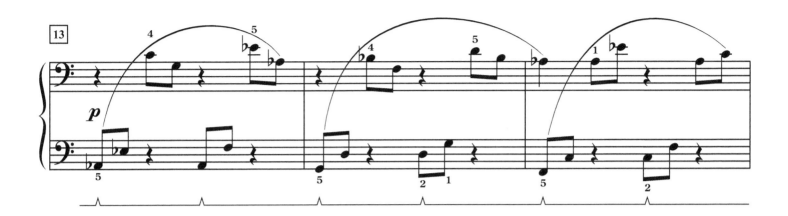

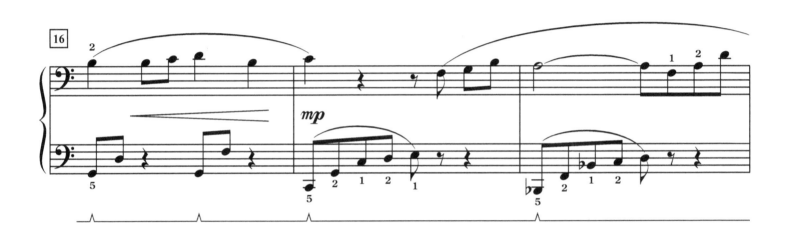

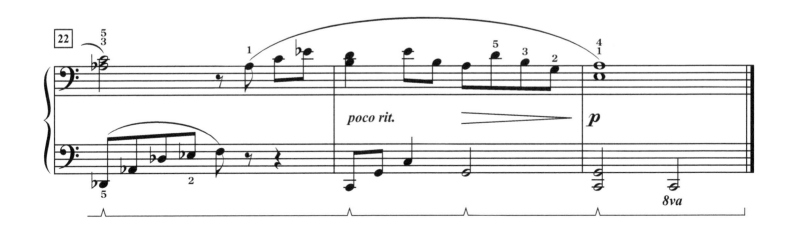

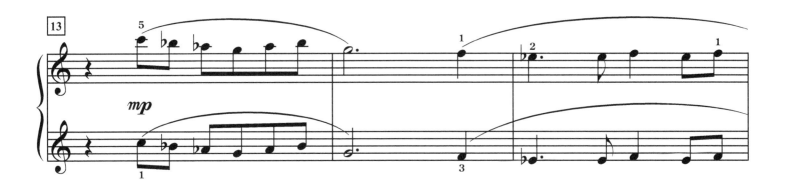

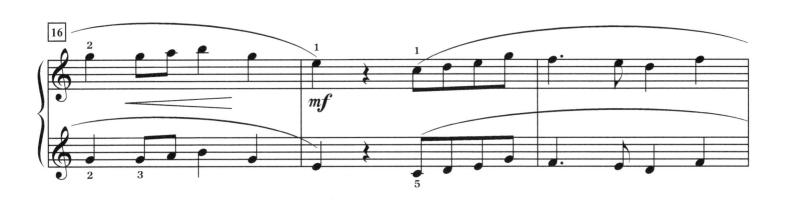

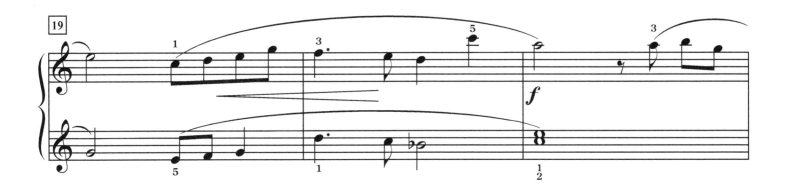

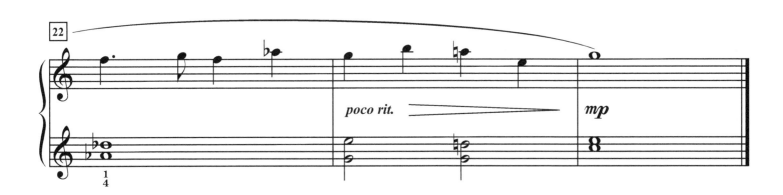

FIESTA FEVER
Secondo

Dennis Alexander

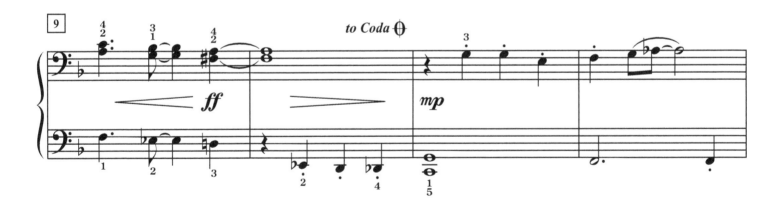

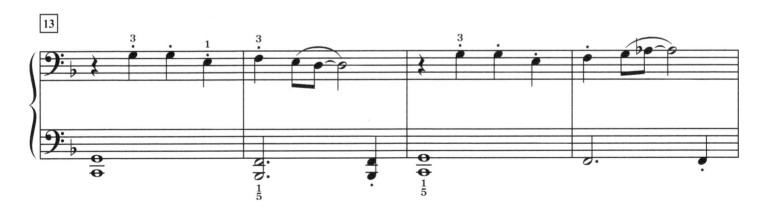

FIESTA FEVER
Primo

Dennis Alexander

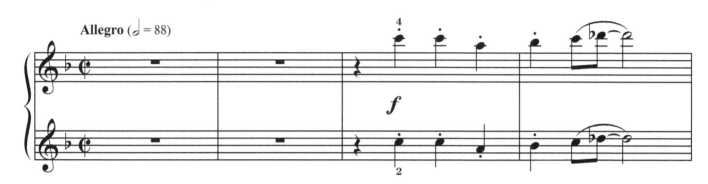

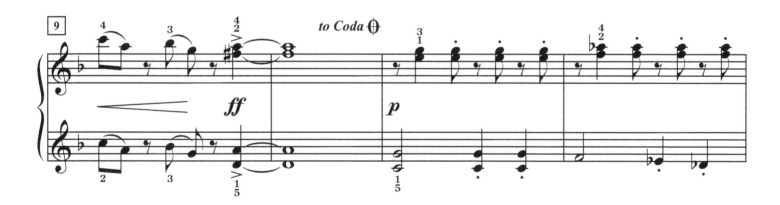

Secondo

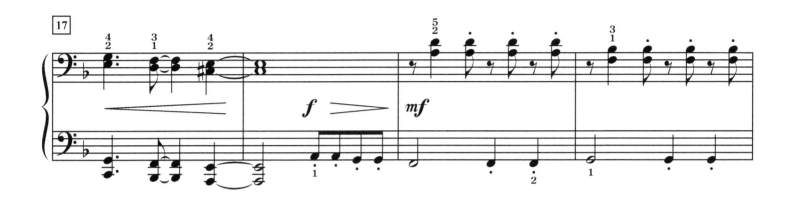

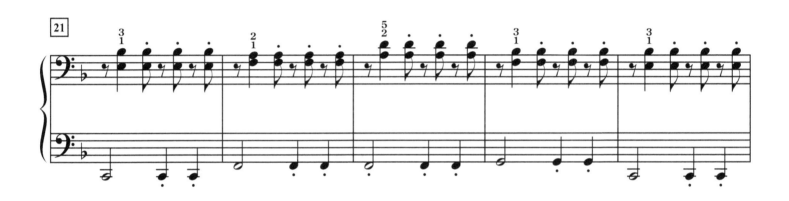

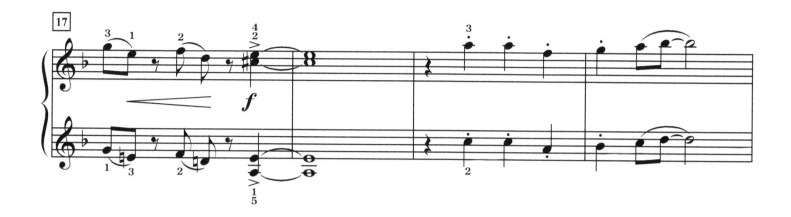

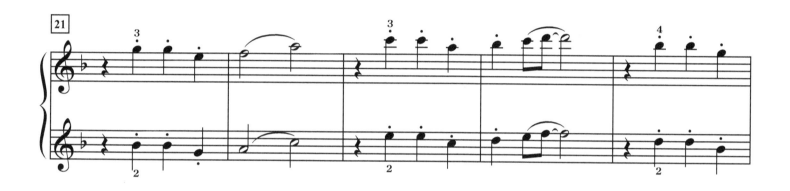

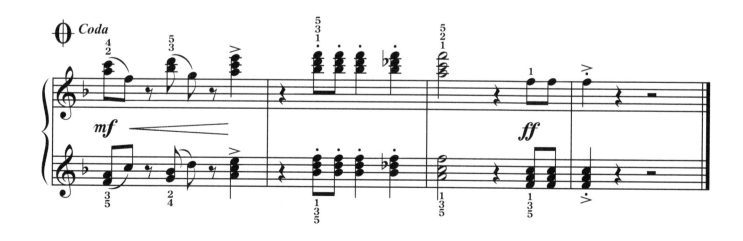

BALLAD
Secondo

Dennis Alexander

Andante cantabile (♩ = 96)

simile

BALLAD
Primo

Dennis Alexander

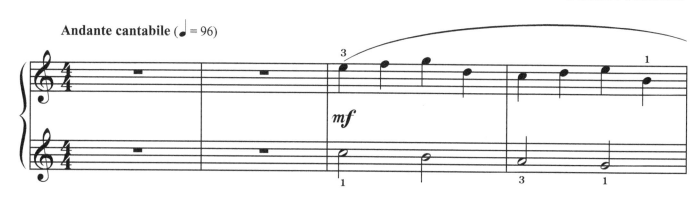

Secondo

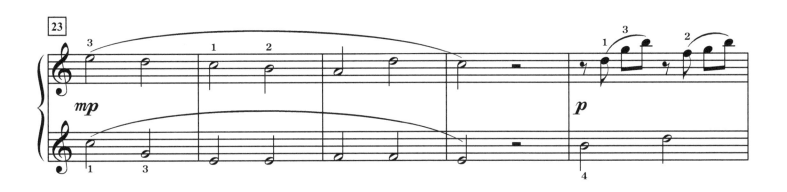

MONTANA RAG
Secondo

Dennis Alexander

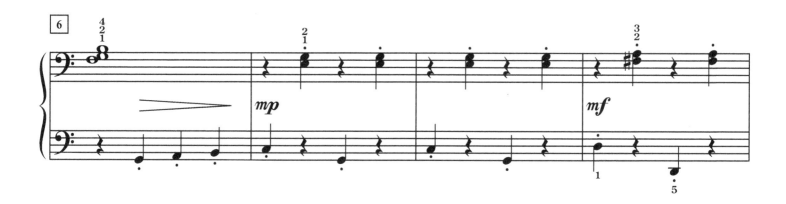

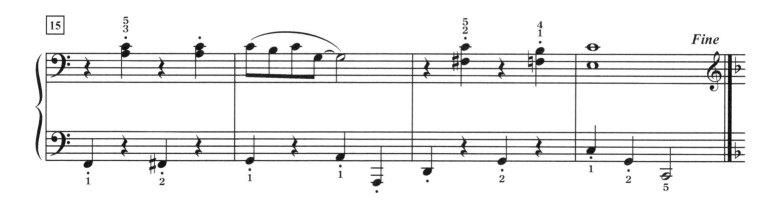

MONTANA RAG
Primo

Dennis Alexander

Secondo

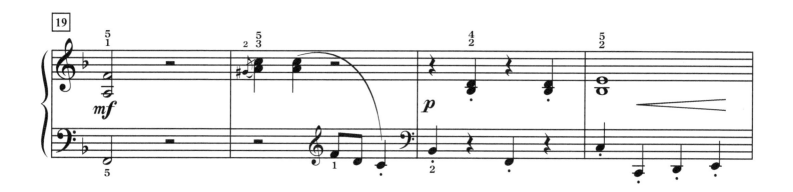

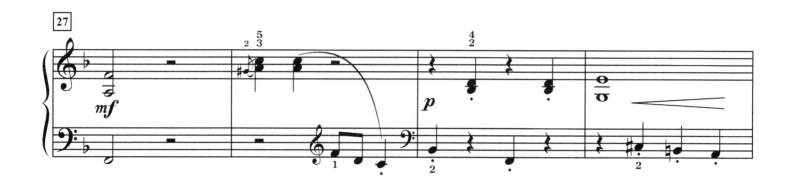

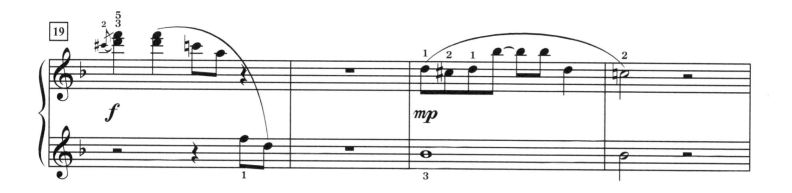

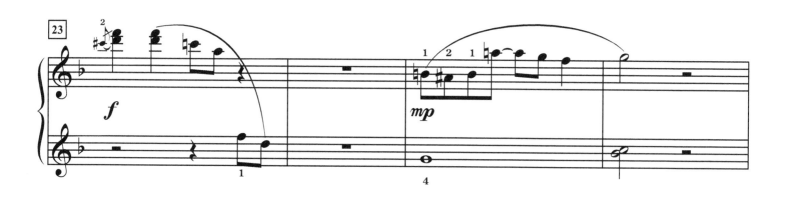

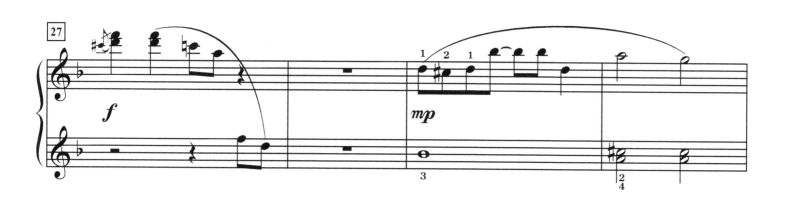

THE LAST DANCE
Secondo

Dennis Alexander

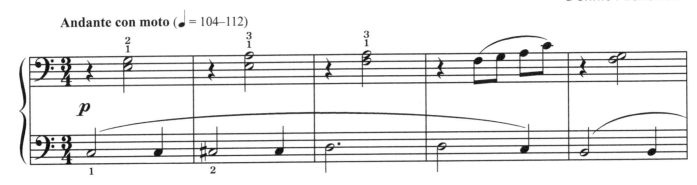

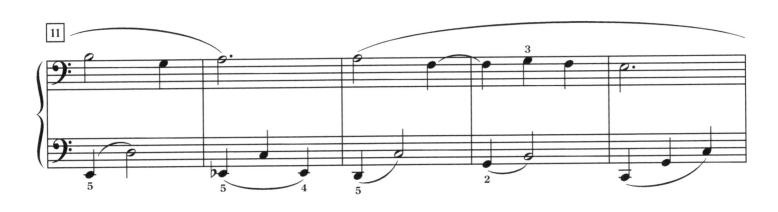

THE LAST DANCE
Primo

Dennis Alexander

Secondo

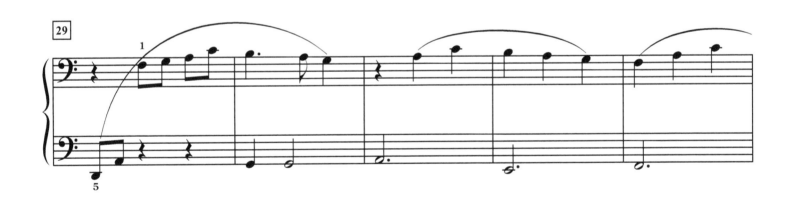

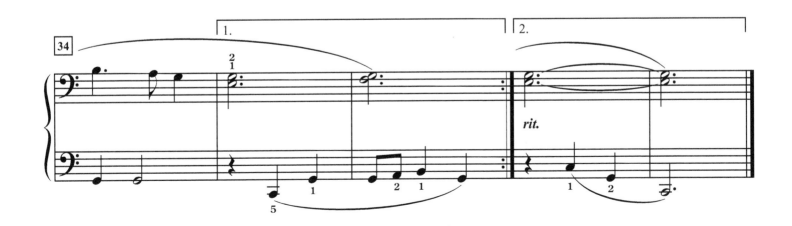

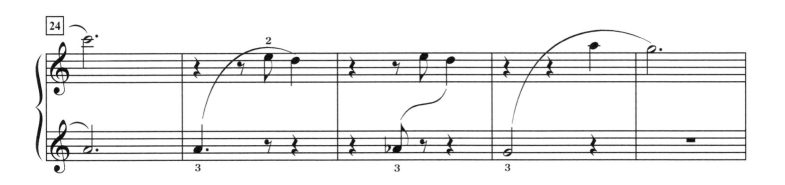

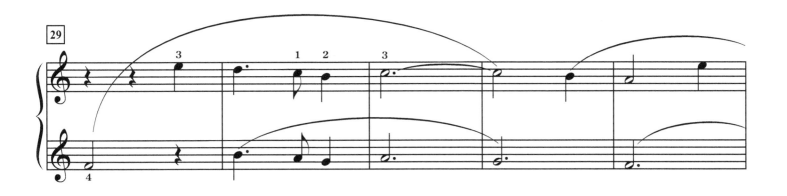

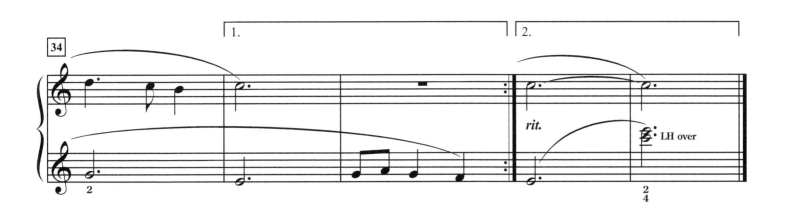

SOFT-SHOE SALLY
Secondo

Dennis Alexander

SOFT-SHOE SALLY
Primo

Dennis Alexander

Secondo

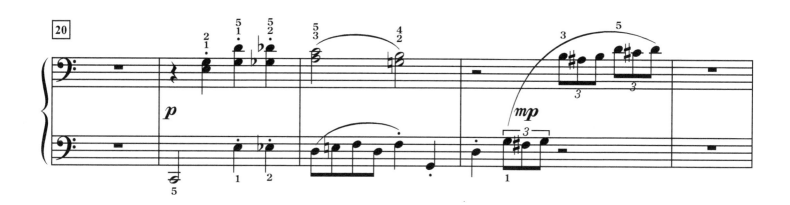

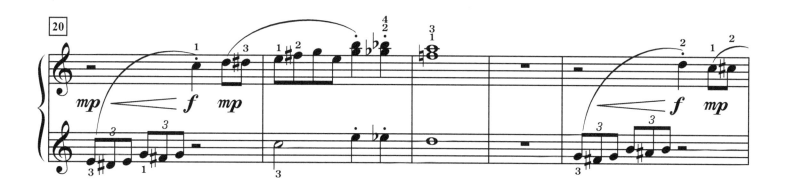

BRIGHT RED!
Secondo

Dennis Alexander

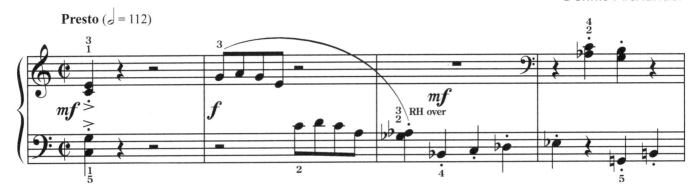

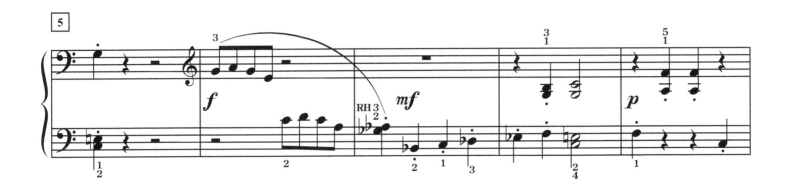

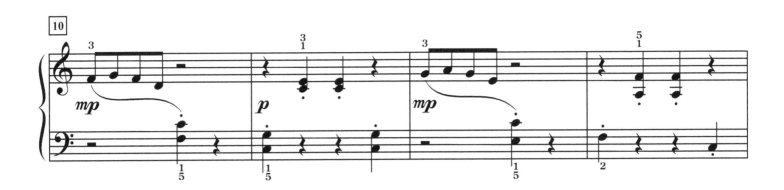

BRIGHT RED!
Primo

Dennis Alexander

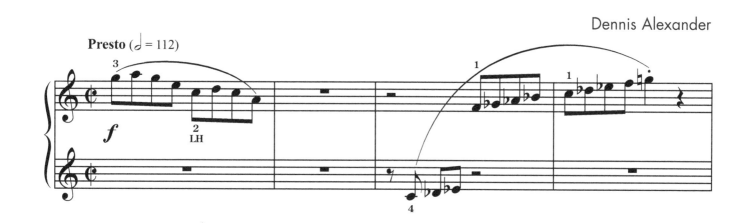

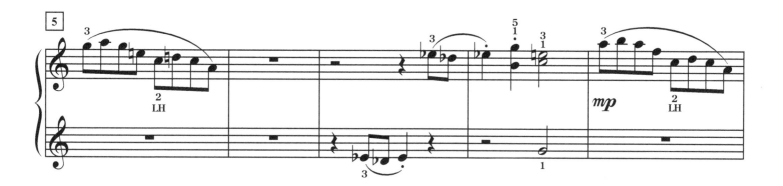

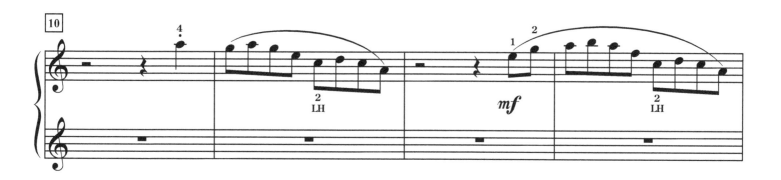

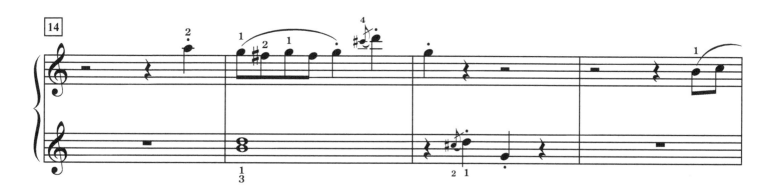

Secondo

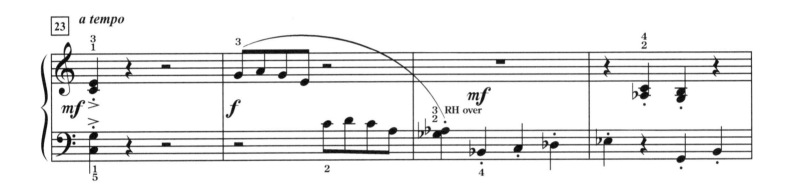

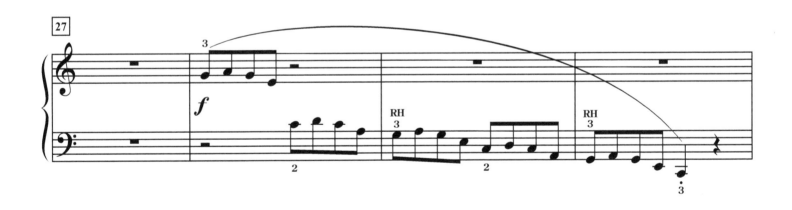

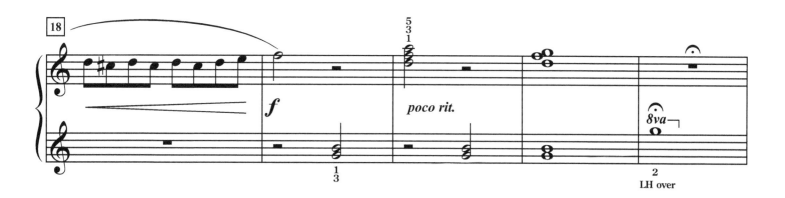

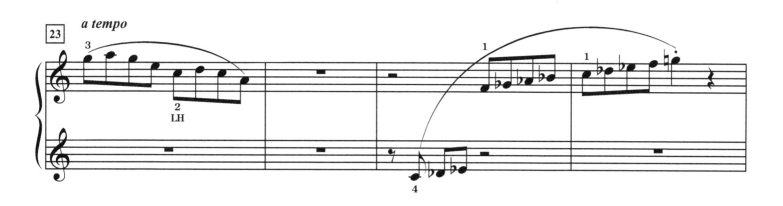

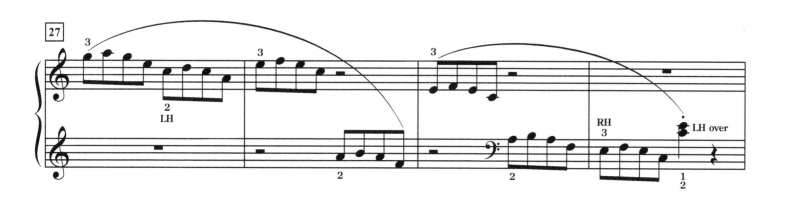

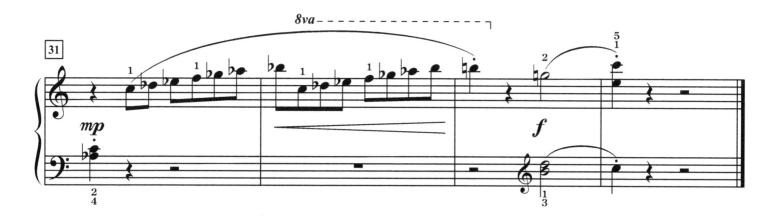

SOUND THE TRUMPETS!
Secondo

Dennis Alexander

SOUND THE TRUMPETS!
Primo

Dennis Alexander